# No More Hurt Workbook
By *Pastor Rhonda Spencer*

# Testimony of "No More Hurt"

"'No More Hurt' has helped me overcome tendencies to be overly sensitive, prideful, critical and judgmental. I would take peoples actions and words too personally (as if I were really that important) and base my opinions about people on one unpleasant encounter with them, not giving them another chance. If a person did something I didn't like (even if it didn't affect me personally), I would choose to not like them at all and keep them at a "safe" distance from me. I have learned to look at people through God's eyes; seeing the value in every person, even those I may not like or agree with. My response to uncomfortable circumstances has changed from asking "God, Why is this happening to me!?" to declaring "God, I know you have a bigger plan than what I can see and I trust You that the outcome will be better than I can even imagine." I have learned to look past the things I may not like about a person to see how much God loves and values them and to value them for what they mean to God. Emotional pain really is optional.
Now that I know these things, I am empowered to succeed in any circumstance with any person." ~ Grateful Reader, NY

# No More Hurt Workbook

**Chapter 1**
Worth & Value

**Chapter 2**
Handling Rejection

**Chapter 3**
Hurting People Hurt People

**Chapter 4**
I Am Not Hurt, Just Offended

**Chapter 5**
People Have Immeasurable Value

**Chapter 6**
Forgive

**Chapter 7**
Stop Reliving It

**Chapter 8**
I Cannot Forget

**Chapter 9**
Communicate

**Chapter 10**
Healed. No More Hurt

# Chapter 1

# **Worth & Value**

What are the hurts in my life that I have allowed to define my value and worth instead of letting God determine my worth and value?
(Identifying is twofold, it will help prevent future mistakes and more hurt, plus it will enable you to let go of the pain and release those people of responsibility.)

_____
_____
_____
_____

What are the areas of my life that I feel so good about myself in that my self worth has become rooted in those things, instead of in God?
(Would I be hurt if those things were gone tomorrow? How can I shift my thinking to make sure I will not be moved without those things/people in my life?)

_____
_____
_____
_____

> **THE MOST POWERFUL VOICE IN MY LIFE IS GOD'S WORD. HE DIED FOR ME, HE SAVED ME, HE RANSOMED ME. YOU'VE DONE NONE OF THOSE THINGS FOR ME, SO PLEASE DON'T MIND IF I AM NOT MOVED OR DEFINED BY YOUR WORDS.**

Write out scriptures that will build your faith in God, that will keep your shield up so that nothing can come in and hurt you anymore. Scriptures are included at the end of this chapter. You can circle or highlight them and come back to them for reference. Your faith will increase when you study the scriptures on who God says you are.

_____
_____
_____
_____

Determine a specific time that you will get into the Word of God every day. Start today and be consistent and committed. You cannot live a successful Christian life without the Word of God. _____ am/ pm.

What thoughts do I have that are causing me hurt today; thoughts that cause me to be dissatisfied, disgruntled and in strife?

_____
_____
_____
_____

Cast down these thoughts and teach them to obey the Word of God.

# My Personal Journal
## (someday this will serve as a reminder of your victories)

_____
_____
_____
_____
_____
_____
_____

Joshua 1:8 (NIV)
"Keep this Book of the Law always on your lips; meditate on it day and night, so that you may be careful to do everything written in it. Then you will be prosperous and successful."

Psalm 119:165( KJV)
"Great peace have they which love thy law: and nothing shall offend them." This Scripture contains both a promise and a condition. It is one of those "if ____, then ____" verses. If I love God's Word (the condition), then nothing will be able to offend me (the promise)!

Psalms 43:5 (NKJV)
"Why are you cast down, O my soul? And why are you disquieted within me? Hope in God; For I shall yet praise Him, The help of my countenance and my God."

John 16:33 (AMP)
"I have told you these things, so that in Me you may have [perfect] peace and confidence. In the world you have tribulation and trials and distress and frustration; but be of good cheer [take courage; be confident, certain, undaunted]! For I have overcome the world. [I have deprived it of power to harm you and have conquered it for you.]"

Romans 8:28 (VOICE)
"We are confident that God is able to orchestrate everything to work toward something good and beautiful when we love Him and accept His invitation to live according to His plan." He knew we would have troubles and knew life would not be perfectly...no matter what could or does go wrong, it is no surprise to Him - He promised each of us that He will always bring us through and out on top!

Psalm 46:1-5, 10, 11 (AMP)
"GOD IS our Refuge and Strength [mighty and impenetrable to temptation], a very present and well-proved help in trouble. Therefore we will not fear, though the earth should change and though the mountains be shaken into the midst of the seas, Selah [pause, and calmly think of that]! There is a river whose streams shall make glad the city of God, the holy place of the tabernacles of the Most High. God is in the midst of her, she shall not be moved; God will help her right early [at the dawn of the morning]. Let be and be still, and know (recognize and understand) that I am God. The God of Jacob is our Refuge (our High Tower and Stronghold). Selah [pause, and calmly think of that]!"

Habakkuk 3:19 (AMPC)
"The Lord God is my Strength, my personal bravery, and my invincible army; He makes my feet like hinds' feet and will make me to walk [not to stand still in terror, but to walk] and make [spiritual] progress upon my high places [of trouble, suffering, or responsibility]!"

***When we put our trust/confidence in flesh as opposed to God:***
Proverbs 25:19 (KJV)
"Confidence in an unfaithful man in time of trouble is like a broken tooth or a foot out of joint."

Psalm 118:8 (AMP)
"It is better to trust and take refuge in the Lord than to put confidence in man."

1 Timothy 1:19 (AMP)
"Holding fast to faith (that leaning of the entire human personality on God in absolute trust and confidence) and having a good (clear) conscience. By rejecting and thrusting from them [their conscience], some individuals have made shipwreck of their faith."

Proverbs 29:25 (AMP)
"The fear of man brings a snare, but whoever leans on, trusts in, and puts his confidence in the Lord is safe and set on high."

***When we put our trust/confidence in God, these are the promised results:***

Psalm 56:3 (AMP)
"When I am afraid, I will have confidence in and put my trust and reliance in You."

Psalm 57:1 (AMP)
"Be merciful and gracious to me, O God, be merciful and gracious to me, for my soul takes refuge and finds shelter and confidence in You; yes, in the shadow of Your wings will I take refuge and be confident until calamities and destructive storms are passed."

Psalm 62:8 (AMP)
"Trust in, lean on, rely on, and have confidence in Him at all times, you people; pour out your hearts before Him. God is a refuge for us (a fortress and a high tower). Selah [pause, and calmly think of that]!"

Proverbs 3:26 (AMP)
"For the Lord shall be your confidence, firm and strong, and shall keep your foot from being caught [in a trap or some hidden danger]."

Proverbs 14:26 (AMP)
"In the reverent and worshipful fear of the Lord there is strong confidence, and His children shall always have a place of refuge."

Jeremiah 17:7 (AMP)
"[Most] blessed is the man who believes in, trusts in, and relies on the Lord, and whose hope and confidence the Lord is."

Mark 5:34 (AMP)
"And He said to her, 'Daughter, your faith (your trust and confidence in Me, springing from faith in God) has restored you to health. Go in (into) peace and be continually healed and freed from your [distressing bodily] disease.'"

Luke 5:20 (AMP)
"And when He saw [their confidence in Him, springing from] their faith, He said, 'Man, your sins are forgiven you!'"

Luke 8:48 (AMP)
"And He said to her, 'Daughter, your faith (your confidence and trust in Me) has made you well! Go (enter) into peace (untroubled, undisturbed well-being).'"

Luke 17:6 (AMP)
"And the Lord answered, 'If you had faith (trust and confidence in God) even [so small] like a grain of mustard seed, you could say to this mulberry tree, "Be pulled up by the roots, and be planted in the sea," and it would obey you.'"

Hebrews 3:6 (AMP)
"But Christ (the Messiah) was faithful over His [own Father's] house as a Son [and Master of it]. And it is we who are [now members] of this house, if we hold fast and firm to the end our joyful and exultant confidence and sense of triumph in our hope [in Christ]."

Hebrews 3:14 (AMP)
"For we have become fellows with Christ (the Messiah) and share in all He has for us, if only we hold our first newborn confidence and original assured expectation [in virtue of which we are believers] firm and unshaken to the end."

Hebrews 6:11-13 (AMP)
"But we do [strongly and earnestly] desire for each of you to show the same diligence and sincerity [all the way through] in realizing and enjoying the full assurance and development of [your] hope until the end, in order that you may not grow disinterested and become [spiritual] sluggards, but imitators, behaving as do those who through faith (by their leaning of the entire personality on God in Christ in absolute trust and confidence in His power, wisdom, and goodness) and by practice of patient endurance and waiting are [now] inheriting the promises.
For when God made [His] promise to Abraham, He swore by Himself, since He had no one greater by whom to swear."

Hebrews 10:35 (AMP)
"Do not, therefore, fling away your fearless confidence, for it carries a great and glorious compensation of reward."

2 Peter 3:14 (AMP)
"So, beloved, since you are expecting these things, be eager to be found by Him [at His coming] without spot or blemish and at peace [in serene confidence, free from fears and agitating passions and moral conflicts]."

1 John 2:28 (AMP)
"And now, little children, abide (live, remain permanently) in Him, so that when He is made visible, we may have and enjoy perfect confidence (boldness, assurance) and not be ashamed and shrink from Him at His coming."

1 Samuel 2:2 (AMP)
"There is none holy like the Lord, there is none besides You; there is no Rock like our God."

2 Samuel 22:1-3 (AMP)
"My God, my Rock, in Him will I take refuge; my Shield and the Horn of my salvation; my Stronghold and my Refuge, my Savior."

Psalm 27:5 (AMP)
"For in the day of trouble He will hide me in His

shelter; in the secret place of His tabernacle will He hide me; He will set me high upon a rock."

Psalm 40:2 (AMP)
"He drew me up out of a horrible pit [a pit of tumult and of destruction], out of the miry clay (froth and slime), and set my feet upon a rock, steadying my steps and establishing my goings."

Psalm 62:2 & 7 (AMP)
"He only is my Rock and my Salvation, my Defense and my Fortress, I shall not be greatly moved. With God rests my salvation and my glory; He is my Rock of unyielding strength and impenetrable hardness, and my refuge is in God!"

Matthew 7:24-25 (AMP)
"'So everyone who hears these words of Mine and acts upon them [obeying them] will be like a sensible (prudent, practical, wise) man who built his house upon the rock. And the rain fell and the floods came and the winds blew and beat against that house; yet it did not fall, because it had been founded on the rock.'"

2 Corinthians 12:9 (AMP paraphrased)
"God's grace (your power for a living) it is enough for you.

Ecclesiastes 9:4 (AMP paraphrased)
"As long as you are in the land of the living there is hope."

James 3:2 (WBT paraphrased)
"If a man can control his tongue he can control his whole body."

1 Timothy 1:5-7 (AMPC)
"Whereas the object and purpose of our instruction and charge is love, which springs from a pure heart and a good (clear) conscience and sincere (unfeigned) faith. But certain individuals have missed the mark on this very matter [and] have wandered away into vain arguments and discussions and purposeless talk."

# Chapter 2

# **Handling Rejection**

What things am I doing for the acceptance and approval of people rather than doing them **only** for God? (Remember not to trust your own mind, it is deceitful.
Be honest with yourself.)
Check your motive: "Am I doing this to please God alone?"

_____
_____
_____
_____

In what ways have you found yourself willing to compromise, willing to do whatever you have to do to be accepted?

_____
_____
_____
_____

Do you fear rejection? By whom?

_____
_____
_____
_____

^^Remember <u>when you fear</u> you give that person/thing control over your life^^

Who have I been holding unrealistic expectations of?
Who do I easily become angry with?

_____
_____
_____
_____
_____

Declare this: "I **choose** to let them off the hook and allow them to be human and fallible, because **I know** I am human and fallible too."

Write out scriptures that will help you know you are accepted and that nothing can separate you from the love of God. Scriptures are included at the end of this chapter, you can circle or highlight them and come back to them for reference.
It will help you to do your own scripture study on acceptance and God's unconditional love for you.

_____
_____
_____
_____
_____
_____
_____

My Personal Journal
(someday this will serve as a reminder of your victories)

_____
_____
_____
_____
_____
_____

Romans 11:1 (NASB)
"I say then, God has not rejected His people, has He? May it never be!"

Acts 10:34-35 (NASB)
"Opening his mouth, Peter said: 'I most certainly understand now that God is not one to show partiality, but in every nation the man who fears Him and does what is right is welcome to Him.'"

Ephesians 1:5 (NLT)
"God decided in advance to adopt us into his own family by bringing us to himself through Jesus Christ. This is what he wanted to do, and it gave him great pleasure."

Psalm 27:10 (ESV)
"For my father and my mother have forsaken me, but the Lord will take me in."

Philippians 3:3-14 (Amp)
"For we [Christians] are the true circumcision, who worship God in spirit and by the Spirit of God and exult and glory and pride ourselves in Jesus Christ, and put no confidence or dependence [on what we are] in the flesh and on outward privileges and physical advantages and external appearances—Though for myself I have [at least grounds] to rely on the flesh. If any other man considers that he has or seems to have reason to rely on the flesh and his physical and outward advantages, I have still more!
Circumcised when I was eight days old, of the race of Israel, of the tribe of Benjamin, a Hebrew [and the son] of Hebrews; as to the observance of the Law I was of [the party of] the Pharisees,
As to my zeal, I was a persecutor of the church, and by the Law's standard of righteousness (supposed justice, uprightness, and right standing with God) I was proven to be blameless and no fault was found with me. But whatever former things I had that might have been gains to me, I have come to consider as [one combined] loss for Christ's sake. Yes, furthermore, I count everything as loss compared to the possession of the priceless privilege (the overwhelming preciousness, the surpassing worth, and supreme advantage) of knowing Christ Jesus my Lord and of progressively becoming more deeply and intimately acquainted with Him [of perceiving and recognizing and understanding Him more fully and clearly]. For His sake I have lost everything and consider it all to be mere rubbish (refuse, dregs), in order that I may win (gain) Christ (the Anointed One), And that I may [actually] be found and known as in Him, not having any [self-achieved] righteousness that can be called my own, based on my obedience to the Law's demands (ritualistic uprightness and supposed right standing with God thus acquired), but possessing that [genuine righteousness] which comes through faith in Christ (the Anointed One), the [truly] right standing with God, which comes from God by [saving] faith.
[For my determined purpose is] that I may know Him [that I may progressively become more deeply and intimately acquainted with Him, perceiving and recognizing and understanding the wonders of His Person more strongly and more clearly], and that I may in that same way come to know the power outflowing from His resurrection [which it exerts over believers], and that I may so share His sufferings as to be continually transformed [in spirit into His likeness even] to His death, [in the hope] That if possible I may attain to the [spiritual and moral] resurrection [that lifts me] out from among the dead [even while in the body]. Not that I have now attained [this ideal], or have already been made perfect, but I press on to lay hold of (grasp) and make my own, that for which Christ Jesus (the Messiah) has laid hold of me and made me His own. I do not consider, brethren, that I have captured and made it my own [yet]; but one thing I do [it is my one aspiration]: forgetting what lies behind and straining forward to what lies ahead, I press on toward the goal to win the [supreme and heavenly] prize to which God in Christ Jesus is calling us upward."

John 6:37 (ESV)
"whoever comes to me I will never cast out."

Romans 8:15 (ESV)
"You have received the Spirit of adoption as sons, by whom we cry, "Abba! Father!""

Romans 8:31 (ESV)
"What then shall we say to these things? If God is for us, who can be against us?"

Romans 8:38-39 (KJV)
"For I am persuaded, that neither death, nor life, nor angels, nor principalities, nor powers, nor things present, nor things to come, Nor height, nor depth, nor any other creature, shall be able to separate us from the love of God, which is in Christ Jesus our Lord."

Romans 5:8 (ESV)
"But God shows his love for us in that while we were still sinners, Christ died for us."

Ephesians 2:8 (KJV)
"For by grace are ye saved through faith; and that not of yourselves: [it is] the gift of God."

John 1:12 (ESV)
"But to all who did receive him, who believed in his name, he gave the right to become children of God."

Chapter 3

# Hurting People Hurt People
Part 1

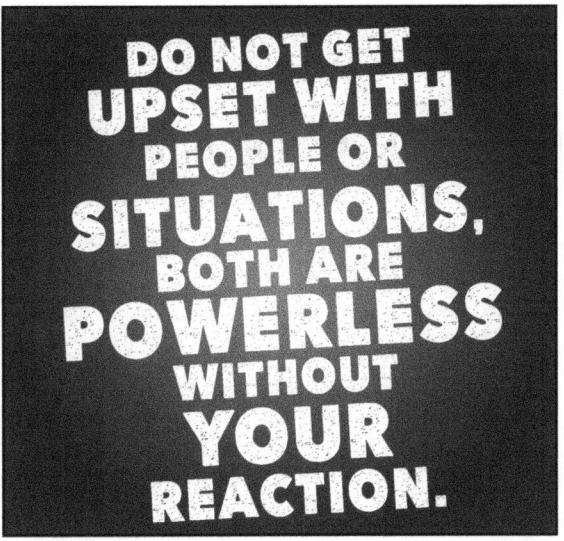

What are my hurts and who are the people that hurt me?
Who do I see as a "bad/mean" person?

_____
_____
_____
_____
_____

Remember <u>they</u> were hurting somehow and let your hurt go. It was not likely a personal attack against you, even if you feel like it was.
Hurting people hurt people.

What hurts have I made all about me rather than considering
the other person's own pain and hurt?

_____
_____
_____
_____
_____

What current situations am I facing in which I can **choose** to become a
peacemaker rather than a part of continuing the problem (believing the best
about others and refusing to put any more wood on the fire)?

_____
_____
_____
_____
_____

Disregard the other person's actions and look at yourself:
How am I reacting to this hurt? How am I behaving?
What do I look like right now?
What cycle am I in, hurt or love?

_____
_____
_____
_____
_____

# My Personal Journal
## (someday this will serve as a reminder of your victories)

_____
_____
_____
_____
_____
_____
_____
_____
_____
_____

Romans 12:21 (ESV)
"Do not be overcome by evil, but overcome evil with good."

2 Timothy 2:23 (NKJV)
"But avoid foolish and ignorant disputes, knowing that they generate strife."

Proverbs 13:10 (NKJV)
"By pride comes nothing but strife…"

Proverbs 15:18 (NKJV)
"A wrathful man stirs up strife, But he who is slow to anger allays contention."

Proverbs 18:2 (NLT)
"Fools have no interest in understanding; they only want to air their own opinions."

Romans 14:19 (KJV)
"Let us therefore follow after the things which make for peace, and things wherewith one may edify another."

# Chapter 3

# Hurting People Hurt People
Part 2

When have I been offended at God because I did not understand why He did not do something that I thought He should have?

_____
_____
_____
_____
_____

What are the storms in my life right now?
What am I worried about?

_____
_____
_____
_____
_____

This is **not** trusting God. Worry is a slap in God's face. Worry is saying, "I do not think God can do it". **Choose** to not worry.
**Choose** to put your trust in God in **every** circumstance.

Sometimes God gets blamed for things He did not do. God is good ALL the time and the devil is bad. Identify and list the "bad things" that you have blamed God for. Shift that blame to the devil (the 24/7 enemy of your soul), where it really belongs, and STOP BLAMING GOD.

_____
_____
_____
_____

God cannot go against His Word that is already established and God will never go against a person's free will.

In what instances has the devil tricked you into looking badly at another person or at God, when all the while he was stealing from you?

_____
_____
_____
_____
_____

What are some areas that I need to restrain my emotions in?

_____
_____
_____
_____

# The Cycle of Love

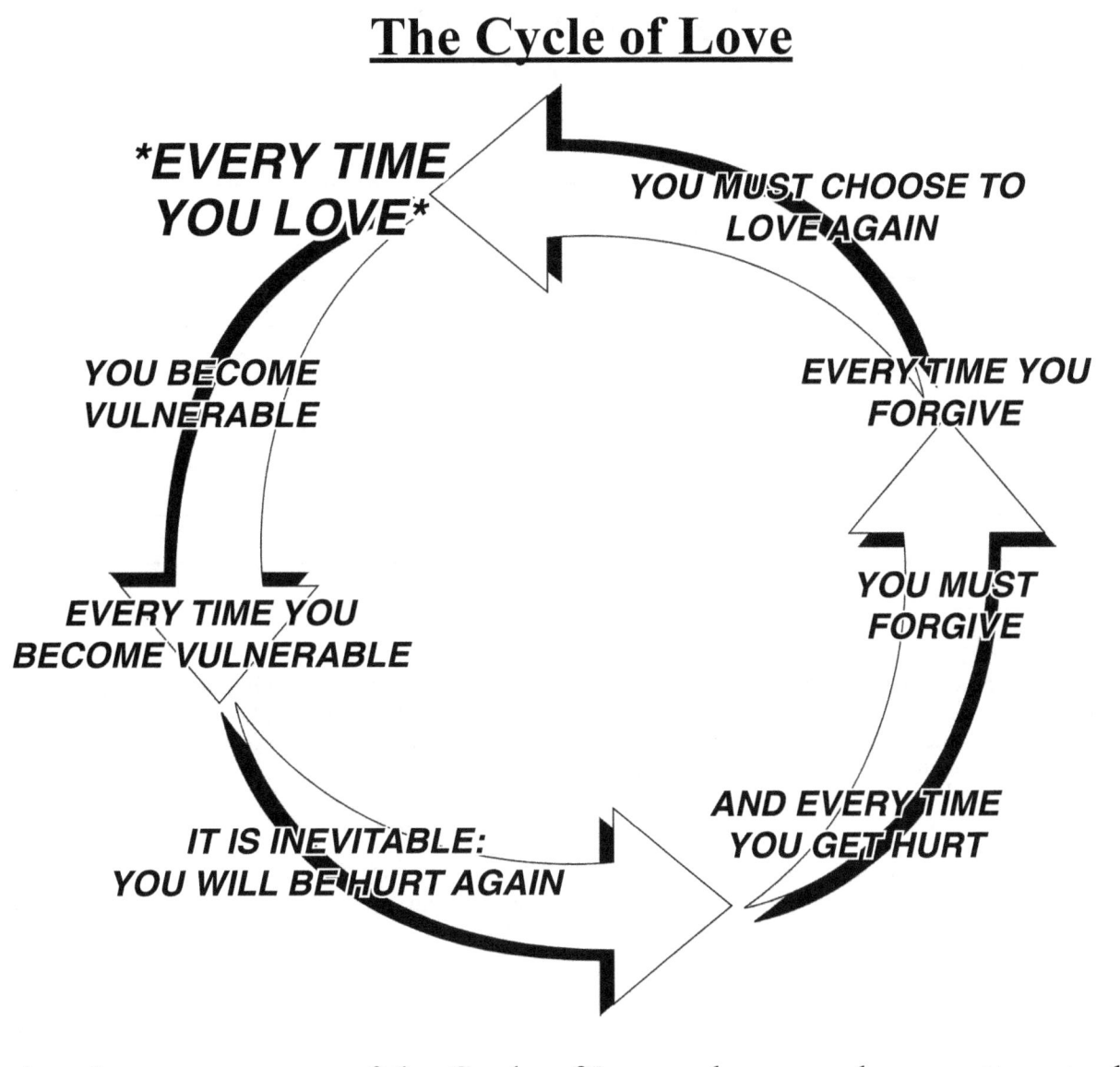

Are there any stages of the Cycle of Love where you have gotten stuck?
_____
_____
_____
_____

Make the choice to move through all the steps of the cycle.

# My Personal Journal
## (someday this will serve as a reminder of your victories)

_____
_____
_____
_____
_____
_____
_____
_____
_____
_____

Deuteronomy 30:19 (NLT)
"Today I have given you the choice between life and death, between blessings and curses. Now I call on heaven and earth to witness the choice you make. Oh, that you would choose life, so that you and your descendants might live!"

Romans 13:10 (NIV)
"Love does no harm to a neighbor."

Ephesians 5:1-2 (ESV)
"Therefore be imitators of God, as beloved children. And walk in love, as Christ loved us and gave himself up for us, a fragrant offering and sacrifice to God."

Ephesians 4:27 (ESV)
"Give no opportunity to the devil."

Matthew 7:12 (NET)
"In everything, treat others as you would want them to treat you."

Chapter 4

# I am Not Hurt, Just Offended

What seemingly "little" offenses do I have in my life?
"I am not really hurt, they are just an irritation."

_____
_____
_____
_____
_____

In what aspects of my life do I feel dry, empty and just not connected (work, spouse, family, children, church, friends)?

_____
_____
_____
_____
_____

Identifying these will show you where you may have "little" offenses that are keeping you from the unity/connection you would like to have.

Where and when do you feel agitated, tense and angry?

_____
_____
_____
_____
_____

You have an offense! Offense will hurt you. Offense will keep God's power from working in your life. It will cause you to stumble and fall away, you will loose trust, betray people, bite and devour them and pursue them with hatred.

Who do I consider to be the least or to be less than?
Who do I ignore or avoid?

_____
_____
_____
_____

How do I treat them? This is how I am treating God.

What behaviors or events from my past still cause me guilt and shame (hurt), even though I have asked God's forgiveness and do not do those things anymore?

_____
_____
_____
_____

This is condemnation from the accuser, the devil. Jesus has thrown these things as far as the East is to the West and remembers them no more. The devil loves to get you to slip up and fall into sin so he can try to keep condemning you day and night. If you have repented, you have no need for guilt and shame,
**<u>God doesn't hold it against you</u>**.

What behaviors do I currently engage in that cause me guilt and shame?

_____
_____
_____
_____

This is conviction, it is from God. Conviction is good; it causes us to turn away from things that will hurt us. Ask God to forgive you and repent (go and sin no more) so He can heal your life.

What offenses do I find myself justified in holding on to?
(I feel I am right and they are wrong)

_____
_____
_____
_____

Acquit, release and **FORgive** them. Give up resentment, let it drop. Acquit means to relieve from a fault or a charge; to declare not guilty. Do you see how this is opposite of the enemy and his devices of condemnation and offense?

James 5:16 (AMP) says, "Confess to one another therefore your faults (your slips, your false steps, your offenses, your sins) and pray [also] for one another, **that you may be healed and restored [to a spiritual tone of mind and heart].** The earnest (heartfelt, continued) **prayer of a righteous man makes tremendous power available [dynamic in it's working].**

What hurts or offenses am I holding on to that I rationalize and
use to excuse my reactions?

_____
_____
_____
_____

Declare: "I refuse any and all offense, big or 'little',
knowing it is costing me too much."


My Personal Journal
(someday this will serve as a reminder of your victories)

_____
_____
_____
_____
_____
_____
_____
_____
_____
_____

2 Corinthians 2:11 (NKJV) advises us to be aware of this danger.
"Lest Satan should take advantage of us; for we are not ignorant of his devices".

Galatians 2:20 (NLT)
"My old self has been crucified with Christ. It is no longer I who live, but Christ lives in me."

John 3:30 (KJV)
"He must increase, but I must decrease."

2 Chronicles 7:14 (KJV)
"If my people, which are called by my name, shall humble themselves, and pray, and seek my face, and turn from their wicked ways; then will I hear from heaven, and will forgive their sin, and will heal their land."

Galatians 5:13-15, 17, 22, 23, 26 (AMP)
"For you, through love you should serve one another. For the whole Law [concerning human relationships] is complied with in the one precept, You shall love your neighbor as [you do] yourself. But if you bite and devour one another [in partisan strife], be careful that you [and your whole fellowship] are not consumed by one another. For the desires of the flesh are opposed to the [Holy] Spirit, and the [desires of the] Spirit are opposed to the flesh (godless human nature); for these are antagonistic to each other [continually withstanding and in conflict with each other], so that you are not free but are prevented from doing what you desire to do. But the fruit of the [Holy] Spirit [the work which His presence within accomplishes] is love, joy (gladness), peace, patience (an even temper, forbearance), kindness, goodness (benevolence), faithfulness, Gentleness (meekness, humility), self-control (self-restraint, continence). Against such things there is no law [that can bring a charge]. Let us not become vainglorious and self-conceited, competitive and challenging and provoking and irritating to one another, envying and being jealous of one another."

Proverbs 17:9 (CEV)
"You will keep your friends if you forgive them, but you will lose your friends if you keep talking about what they did wrong."

John 8:7 (NIV)
"When they kept on questioning him, he straightened up and said to them, 'If any one of you is without sin, let him be the first to throw a stone at her."

Colossians 3:13 (NIV)
"Bear with each other and forgive one another if any of you has a grievance against someone. Forgive as the Lord forgave you."

Ephesians 4:31-32 (NIV)
"Get rid of all bitterness, rage and anger, brawling and slander, along with every form of malice. Be kind and compassionate to one another, forgiving each other, just as in Christ God forgave you."

Proverbs 17:9 (CEV)
"You will keep your friends if you forgive them, but you will lose your friends if you keep talking about what they did wrong."

1 Corinthians 13:5 (AMP)
Says: "pay no attention to a suffered wrong".

2 Corinthians 5:21 (NLT)
"For God made Christ, who never sinned, to be the offering for our sin, so that we could be made right with God through Christ."

Matthew 6:14-15 (NIV)
"For if you forgive men when they sin against you, your heavenly Father will also forgive you. But if you do not forgive men their sins, your Father will not forgive your sins.'"

Luke 6:37 (AMP)
"Acquit, forgive and release (give up resentment, let it drop) and you will be acquitted and forgiven and released"

# Chapter 5

# People are of Immeasurable Value

Ask yourself: "Am I selective about who I honor?" Are there some people in my mind who just don't deserve it; who are those people?

_____
_____
_____
_____
_____

Which of my enemies am I choosing **not** to love and why?

_____
_____
_____
_____
_____

In what ways can I be a blessing to those who hate and curse me?

_____
_____
_____
_____
_____

Write a prayer for the person you believe has spitefully used you.

_____
_____
_____
_____

In 1 Peter 2:17 we are charged to honor all people.
The word for *honor* from both the Greek and the Hebrew means
"to look upon and deal with someone as a valued individual."
Ask God to help you see all people like He sees them.

Who is it that you do not value? Write their names down and start giving them honor today, whether you "feel" like it or not.
Just choose to obey God and honor ALL PEOPLE.

_____      _____
_____      _____
_____      _____

God's Word says where there is contention, that every evil thing and confusion is present and no mighty miracles can be done in that place.
(James 3:17, Mark 6:5)

What person have you been fighting against?

_____      _____
_____      _____
_____      _____

Take your war off these people and start fighting in the spirit realm.
Fight the enemy of your soul, who is out to steal, kill and destroy you.
It's not you against them, it's all of us together against the destroyer.

Ephesians 6:12, "For we wrestle not against flesh and blood, but against principalities, against powers, against the rulers of the darkness of this world, against spiritual wickedness in high places."

## My Personal Journal
### (someday this will serve as a reminder of your victories)

_____
_____
_____
_____
_____
_____
_____
_____
_____
_____

Matthew 25:40 (ESV)
And the King will answer them, 'Truly, I say to you, as you did it to one of the least of these my brothers, you did it to me.

2 Peter 3:9 (NIV)
The Lord is not slow in keeping his promise, as some understand slowness. Instead he is patient, not wanting anyone to perish.

John 3:16 (ESV)
"For God so loved the world, that he gave his only Son, that whoever believes in him should not perish but have eternal life."

Matthew 10:31 (ESV)
"Fear not, therefore; you are of more value than many sparrows."

Romans 8:32 (ESV)
"He who did not spare his own Son but gave him up for us all."

Isaiah 43:4 (AMP)
"you are precious in My sight and I love you."

Matthew 5:43-45 (KJV)
"Ye have heard that it hath been said, Thou shalt love thy neighbor, and hate thine enemy. But I say unto you, Love your enemies, bless them that curse you, do good to them that hate you, and pray for them which despitefully use you, and persecute you; That ye may be the children of your Father which is in heaven: for he maketh his sun to rise on the evil and on the good, and sendeth rain on the just and on the unjust."

# Chapter 6

# FORGIVE

Who is it that you do not **feel** like forgiving?

_____
_____
_____
_____

Choose to **FOR**give, not for them but for yourself. As long as you remain unforgiving, you are anchored to that pain and you are giving it power in your life.

What hurts and pains are you holding on to that are still affecting your life today? (that come up <u>daily or often</u> in your thoughts or conversations)

_____
_____
_____
_____

You **need** to forgive and let go, choose to not keep talking about it. If you are focused on those things, they are the target you will hit.
What you sow is what you will reap.

How can I overcome this evil with good?

_____
_____
_____
_____

<u>Take communion often and always</u>; remembering all that you have been forgiven and how powerful that forgiveness is so you, too, can forgive. Forgive <u>as you have been forgiven</u>, while you were still a sinner. The hold these hurts have on your life will be broken as you take communion.

My Personal Journal
(someday this will serve as a reminder of your victories)

_____
_____
_____
_____
_____
_____
_____
_____

Matthew 6:14-15 (NIV)
"'For if you forgive men when they sin against you, your heavenly Father will also forgive you. But if you do not forgive men their sins, your Father will not forgive your sins.'"

2 Corinthians 5:21 (NLT)
"For God made Christ, who never sinned, to be the offering for our sin, so that we could be made right with God through Christ."

Luke 6:37 (AMP)
"Acquit, forgive and release (give up resentment, let it drop)."

Colossians 3:13 (NIV)
"Bear with each other and forgive one another if any of you has a grievance against someone. Forgive as the Lord forgave you."

Ephesians 4:31-32 (NIV)
"Get rid of all bitterness, rage and anger, brawling and slander, along with every form of malice. Be kind and compassionate to one another, forgiving each other, just as in Christ God forgave you."

John 8:7 (NIV)
"When they kept on questioning him, he straightened up and said to them, 'If any one of you is without sin, let him be the first to throw a stone at her.'" 1 John 4:8 (NKJV)
"He who does not love does not know God, for God is love."

John 13:35 (NKJV)
"'By this all will know that you are My disciples, if you have love for one another.'"

Isaiah 40:27-31 (MSG)
"Haven't you been listening? GOD doesn't come and go. God lasts. He's Creator of all you can see or imagine. He doesn't get tired out, doesn't pause to catch his breath. And he knows everything, inside and out. He energizes those who get tired, gives fresh strength to dropouts. For even young people tire and drop out, young folk in their prime stumble and fall. But those who wait upon GOD get fresh strength. They spread their wings and soar like eagles, They run and don't get tired, they walk and don't lag behind."

Chapter 7

# Stop Reliving It

Isaiah 43   MSG

"Forget about what's happened;
don't keep going over old history,"

**pastorrhondaj** Today is a brand new day, with new opportunities, new potential and new possibilities. Yesterday is GONE, so forget about it! Today has a brand new 24 for you to make something great out of!

What hurts do you hear yourself talking about and re-living?
**(be honest)**

_____
_____
_____
_____

Cover your mouth with your hand and choose not to talk about those things again. Every time you speak these hurts out, see yourself planting "hurt seeds" that will produce a harvest of hurt in your life.

Look up Philippians 4:8 and do an exercise
of things that you should think on.
Make a list of things that are praise worthy. Choose daily, moment by
moment, to think on these things (even write new ones each day).

_____          _____
_____          _____
_____          _____
_____          _____
_____          _____

Do not think on hurt or talk about the hurts.

My Personal Journal
(someday this will serve as a reminder of your victories)

_____
_____
_____
_____
_____
_____
_____
_____
_____
_____
_____

Isaiah 43:18 (AMP)
"Do not remember the former things, or ponder the things of the past."

Phil 4:4-9 (AMP)
"Rejoice in the Lord always [delight, take pleasure in Him]; again I will say, rejoice! Let your gentle spirit [your graciousness, unselfishness, mercy, tolerance, and patience] be known to all people. The Lord is near. Do not be anxious or worried about anything, but in everything [every circumstance and situation] by prayer and petition with thanksgiving, continue to make your [specific] requests known to God. And the peace of God [that peace which reassures the heart, that peace] which transcends all understanding, [that peace which] stands guard over your hearts and your minds in Christ Jesus [is yours]. Finally, believers, whatever is true, whatever is honorable and worthy of respect, whatever is right and confirmed by God's word, whatever is pure and wholesome, whatever is lovely and brings peace, whatever is admirable and of good repute; if there is any excellence, if there is anything worthy of praise, think continually on these things [center your mind on them, and implant them in your heart]. The things which you have learned and received and heard and seen in me, practice these things [in daily life], and the God [who is the source] of peace and well-being will be with you."

# Chapter 8

# **I CANNOT FORGET**

Okay, lets turn this around! What the devil means to destroy you with, God works out for your **good**.
Romans 8:28 (ESV) "And we know that for those who love God all things work together for good."

What are some things the devil has been telling you that you cannot forget and that they are destroying you?

_____
_____
_____
_____
_____

These things **are not destroying you**. The memories of them are reminders of what you have conquered. These things remind you of your faith; that if you have survived what you have, there is no mountain you will face that you cannot conquer.

Change your mindset and thank God that you remember because the fact that you remember only makes you stronger. Celebrate every thing that you cannot forget as a monument of God's sustaining power.

Joshua 4 (paraphrased) "Go into the middle of the Jordan, pick up stones and carry them out on your shoulder. We will use these stones to build a memorial. In the future your children will ask you, 'What do these stones mean?' Then you can tell them, 'They remind us that the Jordan River stopped flowing when the Ark of the Lord's Covenant went across.' These stones will stand as a memorial among the people forever. He did this so all the nations of the earth might know that the Lord's hand is powerful."

Go get a big stone and place it somewhere that you can see it. Every time the devil tries to tell you that thing is going to destroy you and that you cannot forget, look at your memorial and say, "Praise God". The stone will serve as a reminder of that moment in the middle of your storm. It is actually a memorial of God's power and your strength for today and for the future. You are not weak, you are better and stronger. Nothing is impossible.

# My Personal Journal
## (someday this will serve as a reminder of your victories)

_____
_____
_____
_____
_____
_____
_____
_____
_____
_____

Romans 5:3 (NLT)
"We can rejoice, too, when we run into problems and trials, for we know that they help us develop endurance."

Genesis 50:20 (KJV)
"But as for you, ye thought evil against me; but God meant it unto good, to bring to pass, as it is this day, to save much people alive."

Revelation 12:11 (NLT)
"And they have defeated him by the blood of the Lamb and by their testimony."

Romans 8:37 (NLT)
"No, despite all these things, overwhelming victory is ours through Christ, who loved us."

1 Corinthians 16:13 (NLT)
"Be on guard. Stand firm in the faith. Be courageous. Be strong."

Isaiah 43:1-2, 5 (AMP)
"Fear not, for I have redeemed you [ransomed you by paying a price instead of leaving you captives]; I have called you by your name; you are Mine. When you pass through the
waters, I will be with you, and through the rivers, they will not overwhelm you. When you walk through the fire, you will not be burned or scorched, nor will the flame kindle upon you. Fear not, for I am with you."

Philippians 4:13 (BSB)
"I can do all things through Christ who gives me strength."

Colossians 1:10-12 (BSB)
"Walk in a manner worthy of the Lord and may please Him in every way: bearing fruit in every good work, growing in the knowledge of God, being strengthened with all power according to His glorious might so that you may have full endurance and patience, and joyfully giving thanks to the Father."

Chapter 9

# COMMUNICATE

How do I communicate? Is my tone sometimes harsh?
YES or NO

Listen to your conversations. Are they sometimes or mostly negative?
YES or NO

Are my conversations laced with sarcasm?
YES or NO

When you are communicating this way, you are not really being heard. There is most likely a wall up between you and the individual. Do not assume, because you said something to them, that they will remember or that they even heard you.

EXERCISE: Practice good communication for the next 30 days. Shut your mouth more than you open it. You do not have to share your opinion or add gasoline to a fire. Do not rant or nag. Do not respond quickly, if at all, or with negative, harsh or sarcastic words.
Choose your battles and overlook what you can.
*At the end of each day, rate how you did
with 1 being the best and 10 the worst.*

| | | | | | | | | | | |
|---|---|---|---|---|---|---|---|---|---|---|
| DAY 1 - | 1 | 2 | 3 | 4 | 5 | 6 | 7 | 8 | 9 | 10 |
| DAY 2 - | 1 | 2 | 3 | 4 | 5 | 6 | 7 | 8 | 9 | 10 |
| DAY 3 - | 1 | 2 | 3 | 4 | 5 | 6 | 7 | 8 | 9 | 10 |
| DAY 4 - | 1 | 2 | 3 | 4 | 5 | 6 | 7 | 8 | 9 | 10 |
| DAY 5 - | 1 | 2 | 3 | 4 | 5 | 6 | 7 | 8 | 9 | 10 |
| DAY 6 - | 1 | 2 | 3 | 4 | 5 | 6 | 7 | 8 | 9 | 10 |
| DAY 7 - | 1 | 2 | 3 | 4 | 5 | 6 | 7 | 8 | 9 | 10 |
| DAY 8 - | 1 | 2 | 3 | 4 | 5 | 6 | 7 | 8 | 9 | 10 |
| DAY 9 - | 1 | 2 | 3 | 4 | 5 | 6 | 7 | 8 | 9 | 10 |
| DAY 10- | 1 | 2 | 3 | 4 | 5 | 6 | 7 | 8 | 9 | 10 |
| DAY 11- | 1 | 2 | 3 | 4 | 5 | 6 | 7 | 8 | 9 | 10 |
| DAY 12- | 1 | 2 | 3 | 4 | 5 | 6 | 7 | 8 | 9 | 10 |
| DAY 13- | 1 | 2 | 3 | 4 | 5 | 6 | 7 | 8 | 9 | 10 |
| DAY 14- | 1 | 2 | 3 | 4 | 5 | 6 | 7 | 8 | 9 | 10 |
| DAY 15- | 1 | 2 | 3 | 4 | 5 | 6 | 7 | 8 | 9 | 10 |
| DAY 16- | 1 | 2 | 3 | 4 | 5 | 6 | 7 | 8 | 9 | 10 |
| DAY 17- | 1 | 2 | 3 | 4 | 5 | 6 | 7 | 8 | 9 | 10 |
| DAY 18- | 1 | 2 | 3 | 4 | 5 | 6 | 7 | 8 | 9 | 10 |
| DAY 19- | 1 | 2 | 3 | 4 | 5 | 6 | 7 | 8 | 9 | 10 |
| DAY 20- | 1 | 2 | 3 | 4 | 5 | 6 | 7 | 8 | 9 | 10 |
| DAY 21- | 1 | 2 | 3 | 4 | 5 | 6 | 7 | 8 | 9 | 10 |
| DAY 22- | 1 | 2 | 3 | 4 | 5 | 6 | 7 | 8 | 9 | 10 |
| DAY 23- | 1 | 2 | 3 | 4 | 5 | 6 | 7 | 8 | 9 | 10 |
| DAY 24- | 1 | 2 | 3 | 4 | 5 | 6 | 7 | 8 | 9 | 10 |
| DAY 25- | 1 | 2 | 3 | 4 | 5 | 6 | 7 | 8 | 9 | 10 |
| DAY 26- | 1 | 2 | 3 | 4 | 5 | 6 | 7 | 8 | 9 | 10 |
| DAY 27- | 1 | 2 | 3 | 4 | 5 | 6 | 7 | 8 | 9 | 10 |
| DAY 28- | 1 | 2 | 3 | 4 | 5 | 6 | 7 | 8 | 9 | 10 |
| DAY 29- | 1 | 2 | 3 | 4 | 5 | 6 | 7 | 8 | 9 | 10 |
| DAY 30- | 1 | 2 | 3 | 4 | 5 | 6 | 7 | 8 | 9 | 10 |

☆ ☆ ☆ ☆ ☆

When did you feel a wall between you and someone you have communicated with?

_____
_____
_____
_____
_____

Ask God to give you a word picture that will help you effectively communicate what you want to say without placing blame on the other person.

_____
_____
_____
_____
_____

Be aware of your body language. Be sure when you are communicating to include all body language on this list:

- ☐ Make sure you're level with them (don't stand over them).
- ☐ Make sure you are smiling and not scowling.
  (sometimes your face can scowl when you concentrate, focus on smiling ☺)
- ☐ Make sure you are looking them in the eye.
- ☐ Make sure your legs are not crossed.
- ☐ Make sure your arms are not crossed.
- ☐ Make sure you lean in.
- ☐ Make sure you watch your tone. Keep it gentle and soft.

Refuse to fight to be right. When you fight to be right, you lose.
Every man is right in his own eyes.
Blessed are the peacemakers.
Give yourself a star each time you choose not to fight to be right and choose to be a peacemaker instead. Go for a 5 star rating this week.

My Personal Journal
(someday this will serve as a reminder of your victories)

_____
_____
_____
_____
_____
_____
_____
_____
_____
_____

James 3:8-9 (NASB)
"But no one can tame the tongue; it is a restless evil and full of deadly poison. With it we bless our Lord and Father, and with it we curse men, who have been made in the likeness of God."

James 1:19-20 (NKJV)
Qualities Needed in Trials
"So then, my beloved brethren, let every man be swift to hear, slow to speak, slow to wrath; for the wrath of man does not produce the righteousness of God."

Proverbs 12:25 (ESV) "Anxiety in a man's heart weighs him down, but a goodword makes him glad."

Proverbs 25:11 (ESV)
"A word fitly spoken is like apples of gold in a setting of silver."

Matthew 12:37 (ESV)
"'For by your words you will be justified, and by your words you will be condemned.'"

Ephesians 4:29 (ESV)
"Let no corrupting talk come out of your mouths, but only such as is good for building up, as fits the occasion, that it may give grace to those who hear it."

# Chapter 10

## Healed. NO MORE HURT

NOTHING has the ability in your life to hurt you, by any means.

> Proverbs 1
>
> 33 But all who listen to me will live in peace, untroubled by fear of harm.

Commit to do the following:

1. Know you have been given authority over all the power of the enemy. Luke 10:19 says, "Behold, I give you the authority over all the power of the enemy, and nothing shall by any means hurt you."

2. Pay attention to your own reactions to people and situations. Ask yourself, "What am I feeling, and why am I feeling this way?" Listen to yourself. What is the conversation going on in your mind? Does it sound like "the peace of God" type of talk or is it more along the lines of defensiveness and frustration? Once you have identified the thinking that has exalted itself over the way God would have you think, *simply refuse to believe those thoughts OR listen to those thoughts.* If we are holding what other people say as truth and valuing it, we are making them above God. We must regard what

God says about us as more valuable and important than what anyone else says or does. When you know your worth and value comes from God and how much He loves you, *all fear will be cast out* and nothing anyone else says or does can effect you. You will be solid and immovable.

3. Remind yourself you are accepted by the One who matters most. You have been adopted into the family of God.

4. Stop the cycle of hurting people hurt people by keeping the cycle of love going. Every time you love, you open yourself up to be vulnerable; every time you become vulnerable, it is inevitable you will get hurt; every time you get hurt, you must choose to forgive and then love again.

5. It is not all about you. Other people, like you, have immeasurable value to God. Honor everyone; even your enemies.

6. Make yourself free of the hurt by forgiving them, even if they don't deserve it or ask for it. *You deserve to be free.*

7. Stop reliving it. Replace wrong thinking with scriptures concerning God's ways of processing hurt and offense. Forget about the past and press on.

8. Practice being heard. Communicate effectively, sandwich your words and make sure the positive communication far outweighs the negative.

9. Read the Word of God daily. Get the truth in you. Act out the instructions of the scriptures. Do what the Word says! <u>Refuse to do things the way you have in the past!</u> Only then will you find maturity happening in your life; and only then will you be on the preventative side of hurt!

# My Personal Journal
## (someday this will serve as a reminder of your victories)

_____
_____
_____
_____
_____
_____
_____
_____
_____
_____

Ecclesiastes 7:20-22 (NKJV)
"For there is not a just man on earth who does good and does not sin. Also do not take to heart everything people say, lest you hear your servant cursing you. For many times, also, your own heart has known that even you have cursed others."

Mark 6:3-5 (NKJV)
"'Is this not the carpenter, the Son of Mary, and brother of James, Joses, Judas, and Simon? And are not His sisters here with us?' So they were offended at Him. But Jesus said to them, 'A prophet is not without honor except in his own country, among his own relatives, and in his own house.' Now He could do no mighty work there, except that He laid His hands on a few sick people and healed them."

Mark 4:16-17 (AMP)
"'And in the same way the ones sown upon stony ground are those who, when they hear the Word, at once receive and accept and welcome it with joy; and they have no real root in themselves, and so they endure for a little while; then when trouble or persecution arises on account of the Word, they immediately are offended (become displeased, indignant, resentful) and they stumble and fall away.'"

Matthew 24:10-13 (AMP)
"'And then many will be offended and repelled and will begin to distrust and desert [Him Whom they ought to trust and obey] and will stumble and fall away and betray one another and pursue one another with hatred. And many false prophets will rise up and deceive and lead many into error. And the love of the great body of people will grow cold because of the multiplied lawlessness and iniquity, but he who endures to the end will be saved.'"

1 Corinthians 13:5 (AMP)
"Love (God's love in us) does not insist on its own rights or its own way, for it is not self-seeking; it is not touchy or fretful or resentful; it takes no account of the evil done to it [it pays no attention to a suffered wrong]."

Romans 12:2 (NIV)
"Do not conform any longer to the pattern of this world, but be transformed by the renewing of your mind. Then you will be able to test and approve what God's will is - his good, pleasing and perfect will."

2 Corinthians 2:11 (NKJV) advises us to be aware of this danger.
"Lest Satan should take advantage of us; for we are not ignorant of his devices."

2 Corinthians 10:3-5 (NKJV) *provides directions on how to renew our minds*:
"For though we walk in the flesh, we do not war after the flesh: (For the weapons of our warfare are not carnal, but mighty through God to the pulling down of strong holds;) Casting down imaginations, and every high thing that exalteth itself against the knowledge of God, and bringing into captivity every thought to the obedience of Christ."

Philippians 1:9-10 (KJV)
"And this I pray, that your love may abound yet more and more in knowledge and in all judgment; That ye may approve things that are excellent; that ye may be sincere and without offense till the day of Christ"

Ephesians 4:27 (AMP)
"Leave no [such] room or foothold for the devil [give no opportunity to him]."

Proverbs 4:23 (NLT)
"Guard your heart above all else, for it determines the course of your life."

Psalm 119:101 (NASB)
"I have restrained my feet from every evil way, That I may keep Your word."

Proverbs 22:3 (AMP)
"A prudent man foresees evil and hides himself, But the simple pass on and are punished."

1 Peter 5:8 (NKJV)
"Be sober, be vigilant; because your adversary the devil walks about like a roaring lion, seeking whom he may devour."

2 Timothy 4:5 (NKJV)
"But you be watchful in all things…"

Deuteronomy 4:9 (NKJV)
"Only take heed to yourself, and diligently keep yourself, lest you forget the things your eyes have seen, and lest they depart from your heart all the days of your life. And teach them to your children and your grandchildren."

Psalm 18:33 (AMP)
"He makes my feet like hinds' feet [able to stand firmly or make progress on the dangerous heights of testing and trouble]; He sets me securely upon my high places."

Acts 14:22 (AMP)
"Establishing and strengthening the souls and the hearts of the disciples, urging and warning and encouraging them to stand firm in the faith, and [telling them] that it is through many hardships and tribulations we must enter the kingdom of God."

1 Corinthians 10:12-13 (AMP)
"Therefore let anyone who thinks he stands [who feels sure that he has a steadfast mind and is standing firm], take heed lest he fall [into sin]. For no temptation (no trial regarded as enticing to sin), [no matter how it comes or where it leads] has overtaken you and laid hold on you that is not common to man [that is, no temptation or trial has come to you that is beyond human resistance and that is not adjusted and adapted and belonging to human experience, and such as man can bear]. But God is faithful [to His Word and to His compassionate nature], and He [can be trusted] not to let you be tempted and tried and assayed beyond your ability and strength of resistance and power to endure, but with the temptation He will [always] also provide the way out (the means of escape to [c]a landing place), that you may be capable and strong and powerful to bear up under it patiently."

Proverbs 12:18 (NKJV)
"There is one who speaks like the piercings of a sword, But the tongue of the wise promotes health."

Psalm 147:3 (ESV)
"He heals the brokenhearted
And binds up their wounds."

Proverbs 18:14 (NKJV)
"The spirit of a man will sustain him in sickness, But who can bear a broken spirit?"
(If you are strong in spirit it will sustain you)

James 4:7 (AMP)
"So be subject to God. Resist the devil [stand firm against him], and he will flee from you."

Testify of the areas you have been healed and let the devil know you have victory.  Write them out!

_____
_____
_____
_____
_____
_____
_____
_____
_____
_____
_____
_____
_____
_____
_____
_____
_____
_____
_____

I am healed. I have no more hurt.
Thank you Jesus.

# Other Resources by
*Pastor Rhonda Spencer*

available at:
**www.RhondaJSpencer.com**

No More Hurt and No More Hurt Workbook are printed by CreateSpace (an Amazon.com company) and are available at Amazon.com and other retail outlets

www.ingramcontent.com/pod-product-compliance
Lightning Source LLC
LaVergne TN
LVHW061253060426
835507LV00017B/2054